THURSDAY NIGHT PIZZA

THURSDAY NIGHT PIZZA

FATHER DOMINIC'S
FAVORITE PIZZA RECIPES

REEDY PRESS

FR. DOMINIC GARRAMONE, O.S.B.

Reedy Press
PO Box 5131
St. Louis, MO 63139, USA

Library of Congress Control Number: 2010936462
ISBN: 978-1-933370-65-1

Please visit our website at www.reedypress.com.

Design by Jill Halpin.
Cover and inside cover photographs by Mark Scott Abeln.
Interior photographs provided by Fr. Dominic.

Printed in the United States of America
10 11 12 13 14   5 4 3 2 1

To Kevin Rosenberg ("Give me back my arm!")

and Andrew Loebach ("Bury your horses!")

in gratitude for their many labors as kitchen angels and travel companions.

CONTENTS

SPECIAL THANKS TO

My fellow monks of Saint Bede Abbey, for being willing test subjects over the past twenty years.

Chef Charles Robinson of Illinois Central College Culinary Arts Institute and his talented students, especially Liz Steffen, Holly Phillips, and John Wald for their professional assistance on the video and camera shoots for this book and the public television pledge special.

Chet Tomczyk of WTVP Channel 47 Peoria for his support of this project and for his friendship.

Mark Abeln for his collaboration as a pizza photographer.

Adisa Kalkan of Volpi Meats, Inc., for providing me with a wide variety of Italian meats and cheeses to play with in the kitchen.

Kevin Ryan and Sharon Pannenburg of the Nodding Onion, for sharing their restaurant and their creativity in developing new recipes and menus for pizza parties.

The Saint Bede Academy Stage Rats for processing hundreds of pounds of tomatoes for sauce, chopping vegetables, cooking sausage, weighing dough, waiting tables, cleaning counters, washing dishes, and doing all the jobs I don't feel like doing.

Jim Chamberlain for being my #1 pizza fan.

PIZZA BASICS

WHY THURSDAY NIGHT?

A lot of my friends tell me that Friday night is pizza night in their homes. It's the end of the work week, maybe it's payday, and you want to splurge on a meal you don't have to fix yourself—and you need something fast because the kids need to get to a ball game or a movie. My friend Chris says that at his house, "Friday is Pie Day," and one of my former students says that for years he's been making pizza nearly every Friday using the dough recipe from my first cookbook, *Breaking Bread with Father Dominic*.

However, in the monastic community where I live at Saint Bede Abbey, Friday is a day of fast and abstinence. Not just during Lent but every Friday outside of Easter week, the Benedictine monks of my house abstain from meat and eat only one full meal. You can see how pizza would get excluded from the Friday menu—twenty-five carnivorous bachelors are not going to be satisfied with the occasional cheese pizza!

But Thursday night—that's *haustus* night. Haustus (from the Latin *hausere*, to be filled or satisfied) is a weekly community night with snacks. We sit in the community room and discuss current events, argue politics, trade ecclesiastical gossip, and read the newspaper. Some people play rousing games of Uno and Scrabble or participate in more sedate bridge matches, others go to the adjacent music room and listen to a new CD. It's a way to relax, but also to strengthen the bonds of community.

Because haustus is about community, there's always food and drink. Fr. Matthew stocks the fridge with soda and beer (kept locked up the rest of the week), Prior Michael makes a huge batch of popcorn, and Fr. Gabriel brings up a cart loaded with whatever the kitchen staff has prepared for snacks: cold cuts and cheeses, tortilla chips and Br. Luke's homemade salsa, maybe some cold chicken left over from earlier in the week. About twice a month, Fr. Gabriel brings up just plates and silverware with the promise: "Pizza is coming!"

Thursday night haustus has been the culinary laboratory where I have been testing pizza recipes for the past twenty years or so. Fr. Ronald used to be our pizza maker but was never satisfied with his dough, so he asked me to lend a baker's hand. (This was years before I did anything on PBS; at that time I was just a dedicated amateur with good kneading technique). Gradually I became more and more interested in pizza and started experimenting with different dough recipes, homemade sauce and sausage, and a greater variety of toppings beyond the usual pepperoni and mozzarella. Fr. Ronald claims he is happy to have handed pizza making over to me and can now just eat without having to clean the kitchen afterwards. He also provides a steady supply of recipes and ideas torn from the pages of the culinary magazines to which he subscribes.

Eventually my high school drama students (known affectionately as the Stage Rats) heard about this pizza business and wanted in on the action, so I started inviting them out in small groups to help on pizza night. We make a few pizzas for the monks, which I take up to the community room (off limits to students) and then create a few pies for ourselves. They attempt to toss the dough—often with hilarious results captured on a cell phone camera—help chop vegetables, assemble pizzas, clean counters and do dishes, and in their own way, form community.

In more recent years, I've even expanded into pizza making as a fundraising event. For several years I offered a "Gourmet Pizza Party for Twelve" at our annual dinner auction. Once it went for $1,800—with eight different pizzas on the menu, that's roughly $19 per serving! I've done several "Gourmet Pizza and Wine Pairing" dinners at a local restaurant (always held on Thursday, by the way) to raise money for our drama department. Many of the recipes in this book were developed for these and other events.

But mostly, I've played in the kitchen on Thursday nights with whatever happened to be in the pantry or the garden: a bumper crop of tomatoes, half a jar of roasted red peppers, pesto made from ruthlessly pruned basil or leftover spinach salad, a couple of chicken breasts from last night's supper. Pizza is surprisingly versatile, once you get past the idea that the sauce has to be made of tomatoes and the cheese has to be shredded mozz.

So in these pages you'll find pizzas with traditional tomato sauce, as well as sauces made with cream or chicken stock, peanut butter or pesto. There are toppings as ordinary as sliced mushrooms and as unusual as smoked salmon. You'll find a breakfast pizza that comes out of the oven topped with eggs over-easy, appetizers, hearty pies laden with deli meats, health-conscious crusts heavy on the veggies, and a couple of dessert pizzas that will make you think twice before you eat another cinnamon-sugar-and-frosting monstrosity from the local franchise joint.

But before we get to pizzas, we have to talk about crust.

A PIZZA DOUGH PRIMER

One of my Stage Rats became an enthusiastic pizza maker after he
spent an evening in our abbey kitchen on haustus night. "Brandon
makes pizza all the time," his mom told me recently, "but you have to
teach him how to make better dough—he uses that packaged stuff."
Frankly, I had no idea what she was talking about. Further investiga-
tion proved that she was not referring to par-baked crusts (crusts that
have been partially baked until they are stable but not fully cooked)
nor to dough in a cardboard can that pops open when you rap it on the
edge of the counter (which I once used for an after-school snack that
proved to be the worst pizza I have *ever* eaten) but to an envelope of
dry ingredients to which you add warm water, knead briefly, and then
proceed directly to pizza making. A worse formula for making quality
pizza dough hardly could have been invented.

I have seen the par-baked crusts in the store but have been put off by
their cost, which seems a little high for less than a dollar's worth of
ingredients. You can make your own (far tastier) par-baked crusts the
next time you make homemade pizza for a fraction of the cost (see
page 16). And although I am a huge fan of canned refrigerated biscuits
cut into quarters and fried up as donut holes, the only time I'll use
them for pizza is to make Kids' Pizza Cups, and only in an emergency
(see page 88). Otherwise, it's homemade dough all the way.

People have been making flatbreads on a griddle or hearthstone for
millennia (see H. E. Jacob's *Six Thousand Years of Bread* for a detailed
history) and just about every culture in the world has its own version
(see *Flatbreads and Flavors*, by Jeffrey Alford and Naomi Duguid, for a

culinary survey *and* a delightful travelogue). So it might be a bit of an exaggeration to say the Italians "invented" pizza. But we do know they brought it to America in the early 1900s, and we have been gradually transforming it ever since.

For our purposes, I'm going to distinguish between two basic styles of pizza dough. There are, of course, hundreds if not thousands of variations on these themes, but we'll keep things simple at first. What one might call "American"-style dough is made with bread flour (with a relatively high protein content), uses oil and milk to condition the dough, and has a little sugar in it, both for taste and to facilitate browning. "Italian"-style dough uses a softer flour (all-purpose will do fine) and only yeast, water, and salt as the remaining ingredients. Italian-style dough is also much wetter and slacker than its American cousin. You'll find these recipes starting on page 29.

As with any primer, I've simplified matters quite a bit. There's a world of difference between a floppy New York crust that folds back on itself, a crispy St. Louis thin crust, a Chicago deep dish, and a crust from a take-and-bake pizzeria. You'll find similar variations touring around Italy as well, I'm sure—perhaps I can convince the abbot to let me go on a fact-finding mission! But these two categories are a good start. (The sweet crust on page 34 is completely untraditional and is in *nei-ther* category).

Not only are there differences in ingredients in the two categories of dough, the methods used for shaping the crust are also different.

An American-style crust is rolled out with a rolling pin, so that the dough is "de-gassed" and both the thickness and the interior texture are more regular. American-style dough is also somewhat denser and chewier than its Italian counterpart. By contrast, Italian-style dough is stretched by hand, never rolled, resulting in larger air pockets throughout the dough and an uneven thickness and texture. Italian-style crusts are sometimes smaller, but even in larger sizes are used for pizza with fewer toppings than the usual pile of meat and veggies on a typical American pizza.

More specific instructions for shaping are included following in the section titled "Forming the Crust." With each of the pizza recipes starting on page 59, I've included a recommended crust based on personal experience and my community's preferences. You are, of course, free to experiment, and I encourage you to do so. My monastic brothers have never complained about being test subjects, and I suspect your family and friends won't either!

The amount of dough is specified for each pizza as well, and I recommend investing in a decent electronic food scale for that purpose alone, although you'll soon find other uses for it. Here's an easy rule of thumb for pizza: for a medium-thick crust, use one ounce of dough for every one inch of diameter. The majority of home pizza pans are for a 12" to 14" pizza, which is the standard for most of the pizzas in this book. Obviously, use less dough for a thinner crust and more if you prefer thick crust, and adjust the cooking time accordingly.

Another aspect of creating quality pizza dough is the amount of time the dough rises, and at what temperature. Most modern American bakers are used to seeing the instructions: "Cover and let rise for one hour in a warm place free of drafts." This guideline is designed to produce a decent loaf of homemade bread in as little time as possible. However, it maximizes efficiency at the cost of flavor and texture.

The action of yeast and its accompanying bacteria produces enzymes. At lower temperatures, these enzymes enhance the flavor and texture of the dough; at higher temperatures, different enzymes are produced, which taste sour or bitter. A long, slow rise will produce both a better loaf of bread and a better pizza crust. Peter Reinhart's excellent book *Brother Juniper's Bread Book* has an enlightening description of the culinary and spiritual implication of this method for bread baking. You can see why the "just-add-water" pizza dough kit doesn't produce a high-quality crust.

You can achieve this slower rise by using cool or even cold liquids when mixing the dough, and/or by refrigerating the dough as it rises. The two dough recipes that follow use cooler liquids to slow down the process of fermentation. The instructions also suggest a stint in the refrigerator, where, as Robert Capon has commented, yeast and sugar still have their love to keep them warm. However, the refrigerated and risen dough has to be punched down and brought to room temperature before it can be shaped, so you have to plan accordingly. When I'm making pizza for haustus, I mix the dough when I get out of school at 3 p.m., let it rise in the fridge until 6 p.m., then let it warm up so I can start making pizzas around 8 p.m. You can also make your dough Thursday after supper and refrigerate it overnight for your own Friday Pie Day. Just be sure to allow for a couple of hours for the dough to come to room temperature.

Can you make a decent crust without several hours of rising at cooler temperatures? Sure! I made homemade pizza crust just like regular bread for years before I learned about the benefits of slow-rise dough, and it turned out some fine pies nonetheless. So if you can't schedule your dough making in advance or you decide your menu at the last minute, go ahead and make any of the crust recipes and follow conventional bread making practice: cover the dough and give it a first proof in a warm place free from drafts, then divide the dough into portions to form crusts.

FORMING THE CRUST

The technique you use to form your crust will have an effect on the appearance. The American method produces an even crust with a smoother outer edge and consistent texture and thickness. The Italian method makes for a more irregular pizza with randomly spaced air pockets, bubbles, and blisters. Actually, you can use either method for either recipe—these are simply the methods traditionally associated with each style of dough.

AMERICAN-STYLE DOUGH

Deflate the dough, knead it lightly, and divide it into the number of crusts you intend to make. Form each piece of dough into a smooth ball. Let the dough rest on a lightly greased surface, covered with a clean, dry towel or oiled plastic wrap. If the dough has been refrigerated, let it come to room temperature before use. If it's already at room temperature, let the balls of dough rest for 10 minutes so the dough can relax before shaping. Work with one piece of dough at a time, keeping the remaining crusts covered.

To form the crust, place the dough on a lightly floured surface and flatten the dough with your hand. Dust the top lightly with flour to prevent sticking. Roll out with a rolling pin to the desired size, rotating the dough after two or three passes of the rolling pin to ensure a uniform thickness. Form a slightly raised edge for the crust. You can do this one of two ways: 1) simply pinch the edge of the dough together with your fingers to form a raised edge; or 2) brush the outer edge of the dough with a little water. Then fold the outer edge over and press it down onto the crust. This latter method makes a thicker outer crust, preferable when you are making a pizza with a lot of toppings, e.g., Denver Diner or Muffaletta.

To ensure a consistent interior texture, some pizzerias "dock" their dough, that is, they pierce it all over with a fork or a specially designed tool called a "docker." This step isn't necessary if you don't mind a few air pockets in the crust. A little tip: when I dock a crust, I use the points on a plastic pasta server.

ITALIAN-STYLE DOUGH

Deflate the dough, knead it lightly, and divide it into the number of crusts you intend to make. Form each piece of dough into a smooth ball. Let the dough rest on a lightly greased surface, covered with a clean, dry towel or oiled plastic wrap. If the dough has been refrigerated, let it come to room temperature before use. If it's already at room temperature, let the balls of dough rest for 10 minutes so the dough can relax before shaping. Work with one piece of dough at a time, keeping the remaining crusts covered.

Place the dough ball on a lightly floured surface and lightly flour the top as well. Gently press the dough into a disk with the flat of your hand—remember that you want to leave some air pockets intact. Using your fingertips, gently stretch and push the dough outward—don't press too hard or you'll poke holes in the crust. Lift the dough up and turn it over two or three times as you work, keeping both sides very lightly dusted with flour to keep the dough manageable. Stretch the dough out to the desired size, leaving the outer edge slightly thicker than the center.

TOSSING THE CRUST

We've all seen pizza makers toss dough to stretch it out using centrifugal force, and it's a lot of fun to watch at a pizzeria window when the *pizzaiolo* has some real skills with keeping a crust airborne. This method, however, only works with American-style crusts that have been kneaded enough to develop the gluten strands necessary to hold the dough together during the toss. The softer, wetter Italian-style dough just won't hold up. Many a *pizzaiolo* maintains that if you can spin the dough, it's already too dry or over-kneaded, and even though the cover of this book shows me spinning a crust, it's completely unnecessary for making a good pie. But you might want to give it a try, just for fun.

Roll or press the dough out to about half the desired size, then lay it across the backs of your hands—use your knuckles rather than your fingertips. Cross your hands at the wrists, then uncross them quickly as you toss the dough upward. Catch the dough on your knuckles so you don't poke holes in it. It takes a little courage and a lot of practice, and you'll want to work over a counter to catch any stray crusts that get out of control! If you accidently poke a hole in the dough, pinch it together to patch it up and finish rolling the crust out with a rolling pin.

On a side note, most pizza makers hold their hands parallel to the chest to spin the dough horizontally, like a flying saucer, to stretch it out. I prefer to hold my hands perpendicular to my body and spin the dough vertically. (I'll stop here for a minute while you hold your hands in various positions trying to figure out what I mean. No really, go ahead—I'll wait. Look at the disk of dough in the photo on the cover and that may help.) Catching the dough is a little trickier, but I find that the spinning part is easier. Think of how much fun you and your friends could have at your next pizza party trying to work all this out!

WHAT TO DO WITH EXTRA DOUGH

When I make Thursday night pizzas, I'm usually feeding anywhere from ten to twenty monks, plus however many students might be helping me that night. On some nights you can add to that at least one janitor, a coach who got back late from an away game, and any alumni who happen to remember what I do with my Thursday nights and drop by hoping that I'm in the kitchen. Since I have inherited the "Mangia, mangia!" gene from the Italian side of the family, I hate for anyone to go hungry, and I always make more dough than I really need.

So when I have leftover dough, what do I do? Either I par-bake crusts for the freezer, or I make the Magic Bread.

PAR-BAKED CRUSTS

A par-baked crust is made with the same dough as the other pizzas in this book, although the more moist Italian-style dough tends to keep from drying out in the process. Sometimes I'll make American-style dough with a little extra water and turn the whole batch into par-baked crusts. Since the crusts are essentially baked twice, a wet dough helps prevent an overly dry crust.

Form the crust according to the directions on pages 12–14 and place on a peel (see page 24) lightly dusted with cornmeal; dock the dough. Brush the top of the dough all over lightly with olive oil and allow to rest for 10 minutes. Then bake on a preheated pizza stone at 350° F for 7 to 10 minutes, or until the dough is just beginning to brown. Remove from the stone and slide onto a cooling rack. If large air bubbles form on the crust while it's in the oven, pierce them with a fork and deflate them. When the crust is completely cool, double wrap in plastic wrap and place in the freezer. Par-bakes may be stored for up to three months, but mine never last that long!

To use, unwrap the crust and let it thaw for at least 15 minutes before adding toppings. Then bake as usual. The crust will be crispier than with fresh dough, but you may find that you prefer that. I like a par-baked crust when I'm making a pizza with a lot of toppings, like the Muffaletta or the Pizza Diavolo, because it holds up better. Using par-bakes is also a great way to serve a lot of pizzas in a hurry. Using a combination of fresh and par-baked crusts, two culinary students and I once made 54 pizzas in an hour and a half for a fund-raiser.

THE MAGIC BREAD

One Thursday night I had about a pound and a half of dough left over and didn't feel like making par-bakes, so I thought I'd just make a large round loaf of bread to serve at breakfast. I formed the dough into a smooth round and set it on a pizza peel well dusted with cornmeal. It rose while I cleaned the kitchen and my students did the dishes, and then I slid it onto the pizza stone in the oven. Not wanting the oven quite so hot, I turned the temperature down from 500° to 375° F. I promptly forgot all about it.

As Divine Providence would have it, however, some helpful Stage Rat came along a minute later and saw the oven had been left on and helpfully turned it off. The students all went home with leftovers for their parents, and I went to bed. The next morning at about 5 a.m. I awoke out of a deep sleep with the nagging feeling I had forgotten something. The big loaf!

I dressed quickly and ran down to the kitchen, half expecting to find it enveloped in smoke or completely in flames. To my surprise, there were no smoke alarms, no fire trucks. With fear and trembling I opened the door to the oven . . . and discovered a perfectly baked, slightly crusty loaf of bread that was *still warm*. I wasn't just surprised, I was stunned. I expected disaster and got a miracle instead. It was like being a sorcerer's apprentice who made a spell work by accident.

Since then, I have managed to work this spell dozens of times, and it reliably transforms leftovers into breakfast without fail. My fellow monks, like any good audience, express amazement at the trick. "This is still warm!" they marvel as they cut thick slices and slather them with butter for breakfast; "What time did you get up to make this?" But a magician never reveals his secrets. I just smile and say, "I *just* took this out of the oven."

I also like the fact that the Magic Bread is an efficient use of energy and time as well. Your oven is already at 500°—why waste all that heat? The loaf rises quietly out of the way while you're cleaning up, it goes into the oven, and you've already started breakfast before you go to bed.

Since you, dear reader and pizza lover, are a fellow magician, I'll share a few secrets to the trick, as a professional courtesy. First off, you have to have at least 20 ounces of dough, about a pound and a quarter, and always under 2 pounds. Any less than 20 ounces and the bread will begin to dry out in the interior and not just on the crusty outside; any more than 2 pounds and it won't bake in the middle. It's worth it to make a double batch of dough at the start and *plan* for leftovers.

Secondly, the dough may be a little sluggish to rise if it's already been through two or three risings, so the finished loaf can be a bit dense. That, however, has never prevented my fellow monks from devouring every crumb the next day. Remember, by the time the Magic Bread comes out of the oven, it's monastic-fast-and-abstinence Friday—toast is all we're going to get, so it might as well be made with a hearty homemade bread!

I've never made the Magic Bread (or pizza, for that matter) without a pizza stone, which retains the heat of the oven for a long time. So I don't know if this would work on a baking sheet or metal pizza pan. Also, I make pizzas as a nighttime snack rather than at suppertime, so my Magic Bread goes in the oven about 10 p.m. If yours goes in at 8 p.m., I'm not sure if you'll get the same results. I do know that as long as you have a pizza stone to bake on, the type of oven (gas, electric, commercial, etc.) doesn't seem to matter.

Lastly, the Magic Bread has a tendency to split while baking because the initial temperature is so high, so a couple of slashes on the top with a sharp knife before it goes in the oven might not be amiss. But be warned—if you let the dough rise too long, the dough will completely deflate when you slash it, never to rise again. So let the dough rise until *nearly* doubled in bulk but no more. If it's gone farther, just put it in the oven without the slashes and take your chances.

OVENS, STONES, AND PEELS

Some upscale homes are now being equipped with wood-fired pizza ovens on the patio, with a domed roof and a floor of fireproof bricks. As much as I salivate at the thought of having one some day (I have a space picked out for it, near my kitchen garden), I want to assure you that you can make excellent pizza in the gas or electric stove in your home right now. I usually make pizzas in the commercial roasting ovens in our abbey kitchen, but I have successfully produced excellent pizzas in gas-fired ovens and electric ones, floor models and wall ovens, narrow apartment ovens and those extra wide ones designed for large families. I've even used a glorified toaster oven like they use to heat frozen pizzas in bowling alleys! The pizzas in this cookbook are for the most part baked at 500° F, which is the upper limit for most home ovens. Assuming it's in working order and its thermostat is calibrated properly, an ordinary oven will do the job just fine—IF you have a pizza stone.

As I mentioned previously, professional pizza ovens have a brick or tile floor, so the heat from the burning fuel—coal, wood, or gas—is transferred to the oven floor, and the pizza is slid directly onto that surface to bake. Some home bakers who are really serious about simulating a traditional artisanal oven will buy unglazed clay tiles and line the rack on the lower third of the oven with them. The larger surface area is convenient—you can bake more than one pizza at a time and can use the tiles to bake long baguettes and sizeable braided loaves. However, for most people, an ordinary round pizza stone will work just fine.

Pizza stones aren't made of stone at all, of course, but out of a particular kind of durable fired clay called stoneware. They are usually round, 14" to 15" in diameter, although you can sometimes find larger square or rectangular stones. When I first started making pizzas, you had to get them at a specialty shop or order them from a catalog, but nowadays they are available at most large department stores, discount outlets, and even some grocery stores. The last one I bought I got for a *dollar* at a yard sale (that was a good day), but they run about $15 to $25.

Pizza stones require special care, but they are surprisingly durable. I own four of them, one of which has been used at least twice a month for about twenty years. The stones have to be seasoned, that is, placed in a cold oven that is then heated to the highest temperature (usually 500° F) and then turned off to allow the stone to cool slowly. Follow the directions that come with your stone, which might be slightly different.

When you use your stone for pizza, place it on a rack in the lower third of your oven. A cold pizza stone should never be put into a hot oven, nor a heated stone pulled out until it is cool, as it will crack from the sudden change in temperature. You can actually leave it in the oven all the time, and it won't hurt to set a pan on top of it, as long as it's not holding a twenty-five-pound turkey. In fact, because a pizza stone retains heat so well, it actually makes your oven more energy-efficient. Making great pizza *and* going "green"? Not a bad thing! Make the Magic Bread at the end of the day and you'll *really* be saving energy.

When you use your pizza stone, it's inevitable that cheese, sauce, and other toppings will spill over and scorch the surface. Not to worry—

scrape the stone clean with a metal spatula or bench knife and carry on. You should never immerse a pizza stone nor wash it with detergent (it picks up the soapy flavor) and any stains that form are not only normal but a badge of honor. A blackened pizza stone is evidence of your veteran status as a *pizzaiolo*!

All the recipes in this book assume the use of a pizza stone. I've read cookbooks that recommend turning a large baking sheet upside down as an alternative, but the metallic bottom of a pan is a poor substitute for the porous surface of a stone, which pulls moisture out of the bottom crust and makes it crisper. In fact, using a pizza stone is the best way I know to avoid soggy crusts. So the next time you're at a Pampered Chef party and don't know what to buy or you need to round out your Christmas wish list, go ahead and get a pizza stone.

You'll notice in the recipes that I always give an estimated range of time for a fully baked pizza. There are a variety of reasons for this lack of precision. First, ovens differ greatly in how they retain, circulate, and focus heat. For example, pizzas take longer in the large gas ovens at the abbey than in the small electric oven in the cabin where I go on retreat every summer. Also, the thickness of the crust and the amount of toppings have some influence as well. Plus, a well-baked pizza is a matter of preference. Some people want the cheese left white and stretchy, other want it slightly or even completely browned. You know what a finished pizza looks like—trust your judgment and don't bother setting a timer unless you're worried you'll get distracted and forget you've got a pie in the oven.

Another essential investment is a wooden pizza peel. A peel is a large paddle used to slide your pizza creations in and out of the oven. The wooden surface is first dusted with flour or cornmeal (I usually use the latter) and then the crust laid on it so it will slide into the oven easily. As with pizza stones, peels used to be a specialty item but now are more widely available. One of my students recently got his at a hardware store.

Like stones, wooden peels need a little extra care and should never be immersed or soaked in running water because they tend to warp. Scrape the peel as clean as possible with a metal spatula and then run a damp cloth over it. An occasional rubdown with a little food-safe oil wouldn't hurt, either. John Boos & Company makes an excellent conditioner for butcher blocks, cutting boards, and other wooden utensils. I use it on my cherry wood rolling pin, too.

As I mentioned, toppings can spill over, and you may find that your pizza has been spot welded to the stone. Don't panic. Just use a metal spatula (the long-handled ones used for grilling work great) to loosen the edges of the pizza and then use the peel to pull it out. If you get serious about pizza making, do what I did and get yourself a metal peel as well as a wooden one. Unbaked crusts slide off more easily from the wooden peel, and stubborn pizzas can be persuaded to emerge with the metal one.

WHAT YOU WON'T FIND IN THIS COOKBOOK

I am not a professionally trained baker, nor an experienced restaurant critic. I don't live in a big city with a lot of ethnic neighborhoods and specialty grocery stores. I live in a rural monastery with a couple of ordinary supermarkets in town. I don't like to fuss too much when I cook, so my recipes rarely use exotic ingredients or arcane cooking techniques. Occasionally I'll insist on a higher quality of cheese or meat (the recipe for Carbonara Pizza on page 76 comes to mind), but for the most part I try to keep my recipes within the reach of the average home cook with a reasonably well-stocked pantry.

In spite of living not far from Chicago, I rarely make deep-dish pizza, and you won't find any such recipes here. Deep-dish pizzas have to bake for a long time and are hard to serve and eat at a card party, and since I do most of my pizza making for haustus, I just don't make them that often. Nor do I make calzones, although Fr. Ronald keeps putting calzone recipes in my mailbox, so maybe I need to take the hint for my next cookbook. And although cooking pizzas on an outdoor grill seems to be a hot new trend, I must confess to being unimpressed. I tried it a few times, and mostly found it inconvenient to be away from all the comforts of my kitchen! My friend Nick grills pizzas all the time, so maybe he can persuade me to give it another try.

Much to the surprise of many people I meet, I have never been to Italy, so I haven't sampled the pizzas of my ancestors' homeland. So you won't find any travelogue stories about fabulous pizzas in Naples or Rome or Sicily (although I confess a very un-monastic envy for those who have been so blessed as to sample authentic Italian pizza abroad).

Even my so-called "Italian" crust makes some concessions to American ideas about pizza. But I read a lot of cookbooks and culinary magazines, and what I've learned I've tried to incorporate into this book in a way that is accessible to the average cook.

Above all, what I hope you will not find in this book is the kind of pizza snobbery I sometimes see in articles, cookbooks, and television shows about pizza. It doesn't matter if the "expert" is from Naples or New York, Chicago or the Cordon Bleu. Someone's always trying to tell us that *real* pizza only uses a certain flour for the dough, or that you can't call it pizza unless it has such and such a cheese, or the sauce is made in this way or that, or that your taste is decidedly inferior if you like non-traditional toppings.

To which I reply: "Piffle."

Throughout its long and varied history, what we call pizza has been adapted to every region and culture, influenced by farming and commerce, personal taste and public sentiment, and in a few cases, civil law. The pizza that Gennaro Lombardi brought from Naples to New York in 1905 would have been unrecognizable to his fifteenth-century ancestors who had never seen a tomato, and its gradual evolution in this country has been as eclectic as it has been inevitable. Food fads and culinary trends come and go, sometimes leaving a lasting influence on our personal tastes and communal traditions. Cultures begin to blend (often after an initial clash) and foods cross borders of nations and neighborhoods. The result is a pizza buffet far grander and more generous than any cookbook can contain.

So what's the "best" pizza? The one you're hungry for right now. Let's get to work.

PLAYING IN THE KITCHEN

For the recipes that follow, the amounts for sauce, cheese, and other toppings on pizzas are only recommendations and represent approximate amounts. The measuring of sauce is particularly tricky, and everyone at the table may have a different personal preference. This especially is true when you make your own sauces and the thickness and intensity of flavor may be variable. The spiciness of the local deli's sausage, the age of the cheese, the freshness of the vegetables, the season of the year—these are all variables that can affect the end result and require some alteration in the recipe. Baking times are also variable, depending upon how well your oven retains and distributes heat. So for those people who feel nervous about playing with ingredients or technique: follow the recipe once if you must, and then take some chances!

CRUSTS AND SAUCES

BASIC AMERICAN-STYLE PIZZA CRUST

Makes two 12" to 14" medium-thick crusts, or three smaller ones.

1 pkg. active dry yeast
1 tsp. brown sugar
¾ cup warm water
½ cup cold milk
1 tsp. salt
2 Tbs. olive oil
3½ to 4 cups bread flour

In a medium-size bowl, stir to dissolve yeast and brown sugar in warm water; let stand for about 5 minutes. Stir in cold milk, salt, and olive oil. One cup at a time, add 3 cups of flour, mixing each time until flour is thoroughly incorporated. Turn dough out onto a lightly floured board and knead for 5 to 8 minutes, adding small amounts of flour to keep the dough manageable. Lightly oil the surface of the dough and place in a medium-size clean bowl and cover with plastic wrap. Let rise in a cool place for 2 hours before use, or in the refrigerator for several hours or overnight.

VARIATIONS

CORNMEAL CRUST Substitute a half cup of stone-ground cornmeal for a half cup of the all-purpose flour. The resulting dough will be heartier and have a little more crunch to it.

ONION CRUST Add a quarter cup of fresh minced onions to the dough after the second cup of flour. Try this crust with the Four Cheese Tomato-Top Pizza (page 84) or the Smoked Salmon Pizza (page 100).

NOTES

—*American-style pizza dough uses oil, sugar, and milk to enrich the crust, making it denser and promoting more browning. It's very similar to bread dough in texture and appearance.*

—*Bread flour has more protein in it than all-purpose, so the longer you knead this dough, the chewier the crust will be after baking.*

ITALIAN-STYLE PIZZA CRUST

Makes three 8-ounce crusts

1 pkg. active dry yeast
1¾ cups room-temperature water
1½ tsp. salt
3¾ to 4¼ cups all-purpose flour
Olive oil

In a medium-size bowl, stir to dissolve yeast in warm water; let stand for about 5 minutes. Stir in salt until dissolved. About 1 cup at a time, add 3½ cups of all-purpose flour, mixing thoroughly each time until flour is completely incorporated. Turn dough out onto a lightly floured board and knead for 3 minutes; dust your palms lightly with the remaining all-purpose flour as needed to keep the dough manageable. Let the dough rest on the countertop, covered with a clean, dry towel, for 5 minutes, then knead for another 3 minutes, again using small amounts of flour to keep things from getting too sticky—the use of a bench knife or plastic scraper helps a lot, too. Lightly oil the surface of the dough and place in a small, clean bowl and cover with plastic wrap. Let rise in cool place for 2 hours before use, or in the refrigerator for several hours or overnight.

VARIATIONS

WHOLE WHEAT CRUST Substitute a cup of whole wheat flour for one of the first cups of flour in the initial mixing. Be sure to allow for the 5-minute rest from kneading—the whole wheat flour absorbs water more slowly but also more thoroughly, so you'll use less of the remaining flour than usual.

HERB CRUST Add up to a quarter cup of fresh chopped herbs to the dough along with the last cup of flour. Go easy on the basil and oregano or you'll get a pizza that has a commercialized spaghetti-and-meatballs taste to it, but a mixture of mostly chives and parsley with just a little basil, oregano, and rosemary thrown in can do wonders.

NOTES

—Italian-style pizza crust dough has no oil or sugar and is left a lot wetter than American-style doughs. The five-minute rest in the middle of the kneading process helps keep you from adding too much flour, so the dough remains very moist.

—Because most people aren't used to working such a wet dough by hand, I recommend the use of a stand mixer if you have one. Mix in 3 cups of flour using the paddle attachment and then switch to the dough hook for the remaining flour.

—Don't try using a rolling pin for this dough—just stretch it out with your fingers on a lightly floured surface, transfer it to a peel dusted with cornmeal, then add the toppings.

SWEET CRUST

Makes two 12" to 14" medium-thick crusts, or three smaller ones.

1 pkg. active dry yeast

¼ cup brown sugar

¾ cup lukewarm water

½ cup lukewarm milk

1½ tsp. salt

2 Tbs. melted butter

3½ to 4 cups all-purpose flour

In a medium-size bowl, stir to dissolve yeast and brown sugar in warm water; let stand for about 5 minutes. Stir in milk, salt, and melted butter. One cup at a time, add 3 cups of flour, mixing each time until flour is thoroughly incorporated. Turn dough out onto a lightly floured board and knead for 5 to 8 minutes, adding small amounts of flour to keep the dough manageable. Lightly oil the surface of the dough and place in a medium-size clean bowl and cover with plastic wrap. Let rise in the refrigerator for at least 2 hours or overnight.

NOTES

—This is a basic sweet dough recipe, really—if you added an egg you could make dinner rolls!—but makes a nice crust for dessert pizzas.

—I once used this dough for a deep-dish pizza that turned out to be the best pizza I ever made in my whole life, but because I didn't use a recipe for the sauce, measure any of the seasonings for the sausage, or keep track of the amounts of the other toppings, I have been completely unable to replicate the experience! The dough recipe, however, remains.

—This makes two crusts, so use one for the Apple Pie Pizza (page 110) and the other for Fig and Papaya Dessert Pizza (page 112) and let your family and friends vote on a favorite! As noted above, this dough also makes nice rolls, so you can always use leftover dough for that purpose.

ABOUT THE SAUCE RECIPES

You'll notice that most of the recipes for sauces yield more than you need for a single pizza. The main reason for this discrepancy is that it's difficult to make less than a full cup of sauce, and that can be frustrating for beginners. Also, these sauces have lots of traditional uses, and suggestions for leftovers are included. For example, almost every sauce in this book could be folded into soft scrambled eggs to make a gourmet breakfast. Trust me, once you taste the variety of flavors in these sauces, you'll be making *double* batches just so you can think of new uses for them!

This is how I can tell my pizza sauce is thick enough.

Fr. Ron's heirloom tomatoes are wonderful in sauces.

8-MINUTE PIZZA SAUCE

1 15-oz. can of crushed tomatoes, undrained

¼ cup tomato paste (about half a 6-oz. can)

¼ cup red wine

2 small cloves garlic, minced

3 Tbs. grated Parmesan

1 tsp. dried oregano

¼ tsp. dried basil

¼ tsp. black pepper

Salt to taste

In a medium saucepan, heat tomatoes, paste, and wine over medium-high heat for 5 minutes, stirring constantly. Stir in the seasonings, turn heat down, and simmer for 3 minutes. Remove from heat and cool to lukewarm before use. May be refrigerated for up to 3 days.

NOTES

—I usually make huge batches of sauce for canning (see page 44), but I realize that the average family doesn't need 8 quarts at a pop, so I developed this quick and easy pizza sauce with nicely balanced flavors. In a test taste by teens, this recipe won hands down.

—If you prefer a sweeter sauce, add a pinch of baking soda to take the edge off the acidity of the tomatoes and you probably won't need to add sugar.

—You'll get enough sauce for two or three pizzas, but if you have sauce left over, add another pinch of basil, a little sautéed celery and onion, and you'll have a decent pasta sauce for lunch the next day.

BASIL PESTO

2 cups fresh basil leaves, packed
½ cup Parmesan (freshly grated, if you can manage it)
½ cup extra virgin olive oil
¼ cup chopped walnuts
2 or 3 medium garlic cloves, minced
Salt and freshly ground black pepper to taste

Place basil and walnuts in a food processor and pulse a few times. Add the garlic and pulse again a few times more. With the food processor running, slowly add the olive oil in a constant stream. Stop periodically to scrape down the sides of the food processor with a rubber spatula. Add the grated cheese and pulse again until blended. Do a little taste test and add a pinch of salt and freshly ground black pepper as needed. Makes about 1 cup.

NOTES

—I grow lots of basil every year, which I store for the winter in the form of pizza and pasta sauce. But I try to make pesto a couple of times as well.

—It's traditional to use pine nuts for basil pesto, but I find them ridiculously expensive where I live, so walnuts are a good substitute. But use the best Parmesan you can afford—you'll really taste the difference.

—You can whisk this into a Béchamel sauce as well and use it for the Broccoli Chicken Pizza (see page 74).

BÉCHAMEL SAUCE

2 Tbs. butter
2 Tbs. all-purpose flour
1 cup milk
Salt and pepper to taste

In a small saucepan, melt butter over low heat. Add flour and whisk until smooth, being sure to get all the flour out of the corners of the pan. Cook until a light tan color, whisking constantly—about 3 to 5 minutes. Gradually add the milk and continue to whisk over medium-high heat until mixture is thickened and coats the back of a spoon, about 4 minutes. Add salt and pepper to taste.

NOTES

—Béchamel is one of the "mother sauces" of French cooking and well worth learning, as many other sauces are based on it, or on similar techniques. This is the first sauce I learned to make, following the instructions found in The Fannie Farmer Cookbook, proving my mom's maxim that if you can read, you can cook. If you research Béchamel sauce, you'll find lots of variations on technique and sometimes some additional steps. I don't know what the classic French version is, but this one is within everyone's reach and not too fussy.

—You can change this basic sauce by adding a dash of Worcestershire sauce or cooking sherry, a little celery salt or some chopped chives, a teaspoon of fresh thyme leaves— don't be afraid to experiment. After all, if you don't like the results, you haven't wasted a huge amount of time or a lot of expensive ingredients.

—This sauce is used for the Denver Diner Pizza (see page 78) and the Seafood Pizza (see page 98).

BIG OL' BATCH O' PIZZA SAUCE

About 25 pounds fresh tomatoes (enough to produce 2 gallons puree)

4 (12 oz.) cans tomato paste

1 Tbs. minced fresh thyme

2 Tbs. minced fresh basil

4 Tbs. minced fresh chives

3 Tbs. minced fresh oregano

4 cloves garlic, minced extra fine

½ tsp. black pepper

¼ cup grated Parmesan cheese

¼ cup granulated sugar (optional)

1 to 2 tsp. salt (optional)

Remove stems, skins, and seeds from ripe tomatoes; chop tomatoes into 2-inch pieces. Process, in batches, in a blender or food processor until smooth. Transfer puree into a 9- or 10-quart stainless steel pot. Simmer, uncovered, over low heat, stirring occasionally, for 3 or 4 hours, until reduced by half. Do not allow to come to a full boil or it can scorch on the bottom—be patient.

Add tomato paste; mix thoroughly. (You might want to transfer sauce to a smaller pot.) Add garlic, pepper, and cheese; stir to mix. Simmer, covered, for about 20 minutes. Add thyme, basil, chives, and oregano and simmer for 10 more minutes. Test the sauce at this point and add salt and/or sugar as needed (your tomatoes may be sweet enough; the salt may be unnecessary if you use salty toppings like pepperoni, bacon, or anchovies).

Place the pot in a sink full of ice to cool the sauce. Divide into freezer bags or other airtight plastic containers. Store in freezer until needed. You may also can this sauce in mason jars.

NOTES

—I have an extensive herb garden, and people often ask me, "How do you store your herbs?" "I _can_ them," I answer with a perfectly straight face, which usually elicits great surprise, until I explain that I store all my herbs in the form of pizza and pasta sauce! It helps that Br. Luke grows huge numbers of tomatoes every year, and I get contributions from friends in town as well.

—If you use dried herbs, cut the amounts in half. However, the flavor of dried chives is a bit bland, so you might substitute 1 or 2 teaspoons of onion powder.

MORNAY SAUCE

1 cup milk
¼ small red onion
1 bay leaf
2 Tbs. butter
2 Tbs. all-purpose flour
¼ cup grated Parmesan cheese
¼ cup shredded white cheddar
Salt and pepper to taste

Place milk, onion, and bay leaf in a small pan over medium heat; simmer for 10 minutes but do not boil. Remove from heat and discard onion and bay leaf. In a separate small saucepan, melt butter over medium heat. Add flour and whisk until smooth. Cook until a light tan color, whisking constantly—about 2 minutes. Gradually add the milk and continue to whisk over medium-high heat until mixture is thickened and coats the back of a spoon, about 4 minutes. Remove from heat and whisk in cheese until smooth. Add salt and pepper to taste.

NOTES

—Mornay sauce is traditionally made with Parmesan and Gruyère cheeses, but I find that Gruyère is expensive and often hard to come by, so I use a white cheddar. Swiss cheese can also be substituted. White pepper is generally preferred for a white sauce such as this one, but use whatever you have at home. A pinch of paprika is a nice addition, too.

—You'll only need about half of this sauce to make the Asparagus Mornay Pizza (see page 72) but the remainder can be refrigerated and used to dress up your boring microwaved vegetables for lunch at work. When used the next day it may need a little milk or half and half to thin it. Or use the whole batch to make a rather elegant mac-and-cheese. When asked about it, you can shrug and say, "Oh, it's just a little Mornay sauce I whipped up last night." Try not to sound too smug.

PARMESAN CREAM SAUCE

8 oz. pkg. cream cheese
¾ cup milk
½ cup grated Parmesan-Reggiano
Pepper
Nutmeg

Cube cream cheese and combine with milk and Parmesan in a double boiler. (You can also use a 1-quart saucepan, but be careful not to have the heat up too high or you'll scorch the sauce.) Stir until smooth, adding pepper and/or nutmeg to taste (no more than ¼ tsp. of either). You may also add ¼ cup of minced chives, garlic chives, or chopped scallions. Makes enough sauce for two 12" to 14" pizzas.

NOTES

—This sauce is delicious tossed with cooked pasta, served hot, but you might want to thin it slightly with a little extra warm milk for that use. As with many of the sauces in this book, it is made a bit thicker to use on a pizza. You can add all sorts of flavors—herbs, crumbled bacon, sautéed onions, etc. One of my favorite uses is with roasted red peppers over bowtie pasta and chicken breasts, with steamed broccoli on the side. The broccoli gives you something to wipe up the extra sauce with!

—Buy the best imported Parmesan-Reggiano you can afford—you won't regret it and neither will your guests.

PESTO CREAM SAUCE

1 Tbs. olive oil

¼ red onion, cut into slices and separated

1 Tbs. finely chopped garlic

¼ cup white wine

1 cup cream

2 Tbs. pesto

In a medium-size skillet, lightly sauté onion and garlic in olive oil for 2 to 3 minutes—do not brown. Add white wine and cream, stir to blend and bring to a boil. Turn down heat and simmer for another 2 to 3 minutes until thickened slightly. Remove from heat and whisk in pesto. Makes enough for 2 pizzas.

NOTES

—Once you taste this sauce, you will think of a dozen different ways to use it. When serving this with pasta I prefer it with thinner, smaller noodles rather than thicker, but you might enjoy experimenting.

—Using pesto from a jar is convenient, but if you can make your own fresh, by all means take the time to do so (see page 40). If you have fresh basil in the garden, chances are you have tomatoes and zucchini, too, so it won't go to waste!

—Out of cream? use the Béchamel sauce on page 42.

SPICY PEANUT SAUCE

¾ cup chunky peanut butter (natural preferred)

¼ cup soy sauce

2 Tbs. brown sugar

2 Tbs. white wine vinegar

2 cloves garlic, mashed and minced

1 Tbs. freshly grated ginger

1 tsp. sesame oil

½ tsp. cayenne pepper

¼ to ½ cup warm water, as needed

Combine ingredients except the water in a small saucepan over low heat and whisk constantly until well blended—don't walk away because the peanut butter can scorch easily. Add water for desired thickness. Cool to lukewarm before adding to crust.

NOTES

—There are plenty of peanut sauces on the market today, some of them better than others, and you might try a few of them before you make your own. Many recipes call for more traditional (and more exotic) ingredients like tamarind and coconut milk, but apart from the fresh ginger and the sesame oil, most people have all these ingredients at home right now.

—Since tastes vary, you can add more cayenne for spiciness, and adjust the sugar and vinegar for the kind of sweet and sour flavor you like.

—This sauce obviously goes with the Spicy Thai Peanut Chicken Pizza on page 104, but it's also a fine dipping sauce for chicken tenders and can be poured over a salad.

SPINACH PESTO

Makes 1 ½ cups

4 cups washed, torn spinach leaves, stems removed, well packed,
     about 6 oz.
3 garlic cloves
½ cup walnuts or pistachio nuts, toasted
⅓ cup extra virgin olive oil
3 oz. grated Pecorino Romano cheese
Juice of ½ lemon
Salt and pepper to taste

Place 2 cups of spinach leaves, garlic, nuts, and lemon juice in a food
processor container. Cover and puree until well blended. Add remaining spinach and olive oil and blend until smooth. Fold in Romano
cheese and adjust seasoning.

NOTES

—*A great alternative to traditional pesto, especially when it's too early for basil and the spinach is the star of the garden. By the way, mixing in a little arugula, endive, or other salad greens can give you subtle variations on flavor. A quarter cup of fresh parsley is a nice addition as well.*

—*This pesto is a <u>gorgeous</u> bright green with a fresh flavor to match. You can use it for pasta like traditional pesto (it's excellent with seafood ravioli or cheese tortellini), and it makes an unusual dip for crudités—just be sure to let everyone know it's NOT guacamole!*

VELOUTÉ SAUCE

1 Tbs. unsalted butter
1 Tbs. all-purpose flour
1 cup chicken stock or broth
2-3 Tbs. milk or cream (optional, as needed)
Salt and pepper to taste

In a medium saucepan, bring the chicken stock to simmer. In another medium saucepan, melt butter over moderate heat. Add flour and whisk until smooth, being sure to get all the flour out of the corners of the pan. Cook until a light golden color, whisking constantly—about 3 to 5 minutes. Reduce heat to low. Gradually add the chicken stock and continue to whisk over low heat until mixture is thickened. If a thin skin forms, skim it away with a spoon. Remove from heat, whisk in milk or cream to thin sauce as needed, and season with salt and pepper to taste.

NOTES

—I first learned to make velouté sauce for a special egg dish for a Christmas brunch buffet. It wasn't long before I was finding other uses for it (terrific over just about any vegetable), and pizza was among the best experiments! Try the Broccoli Chicken Pizza on page 74.

—Velouté sauce used on vegetables is often kept fairly thin, but for pizza you might make it a bit thicker—more like the consistency of gravy.

—I always stir freshly minced herbs into my velouté sauce, usually a tablespoon of chives and a teaspoon of thyme, but you might try smaller amounts of stronger herbs like sage, tarragon, or rosemary as well.

Appetizers

ARTICHOKE TOPPING FOR CROSTINI

Light, fresh, just a little different—and delish!

1 15-oz. can of artichoke hearts, drained and chopped
6 oz. roasted red peppers, drained and chopped
1 cup fresh parsley, chopped
2 cloves garlic, mashed and minced
2 celery ribs, chopped
2 Tbs. olive oil
Zest of a lemon
¼ cup shredded Parmesan

Combine ingredients in a medium-size bowl and toss to combine. Cover and refrigerate for at least an hour before serving.

NOTES

——This isn't a pizza recipe, but if you want something quite different from pizza as an appetizer, this is a good choice. No tomatoes, no meats, no mozz, and a surprisingly light, fresh taste because of the lemon zest.

——Crostini, in case you're wondering, are round or oval slices of day-old Italian bread that have been toasted in the oven. They can be plain or brushed with olive oil before toasting. Some people like them lightly toasted with a softer interior, others like them darker and rather hard. Try both and take a vote!

——I've seen similar recipes for artichoke dip that use much more olive oil, but I think they don't taste as vibrant. However, if you want to serve this as a side dish or salad, you can add 3 tablespoons red wine vinegar, or omit the olive oil and add Italian salad dressing to taste. Some cubes or strips of provolone might be a nice addition as well.

BRUSCHETTA APPETIZER PIZZA

An explosion of flavors with tomatoes, herbs, and industrial-strength olives.

Recommended crust: 12 oz. Italian style, par-baked
½ batch bruschetta topping (see following page)

Using your fingertips, hand-stretch the pizza dough to 12" to 14" and place on a cornmeal-dusted peel; par-bake for 4 minutes and remove from oven. Spread bruschetta topping over crust and bake at 500° F for about 8 minutes, or until topping is bubbling. Cut into squares to serve.

NOTES

—I'll be perfectly honest here—the reason I serve this pizza to the brethren is so that I can eat the leftover topping with crostini as I work!

—You can make this with either Italian or American dough, or you can use slices of bread and follow the directions for toasted cheese appetizers.

—I don't think this pie needs any cheese, but about 6 oz. of fresh mozzarella torn into small pieces can be a nice addition.

BRUSCHETTA TOPPING

4 large plum tomatoes
3 or 4 garlic cloves
2 Tbs. olive oil
12 kalamata or Greek olives, pits removed

1 small onion
3 Tbs. grated Asiago cheese
1 Tbs. Italian herb mix

Cut the tops off the tomatoes. Squeeze out the juice and seeds and discard them. Dice remaining pulp and place in bowl. Chop onion—you should get about ¼ cup—and add to tomatoes. Mince the garlic cloves and add. Mince olives and add to mixture along with cheese, herb mix, and olive oil. Mix well, cover, and refrigerate until use. Makes enough topping for two medium-size pizzas, or for bruschetta for 6.

NOTES

—As should be obvious from the title, you can use this to make bruschetta, as a dip for crostini, or even as an amazing condiment for burgers on the grill.

—It is absolutely essential to have flavorful tomatoes for this recipe, and so I rarely make it in the winter or early spring. But you can make the flavor pop by adding 3 or 4 Tbs. of chopped sun-dried tomatoes, too.

—Seems like a lot of garlic, I know—but just go with me on this one!

—You can substitute black olives for the Greek or kalamata, but the result is not as good. The same is true of the cheese—substitute Parmesan for Asiago only if you must.

—Use any Italian herb mix you like, commercial or homemade. Here's the one I prefer:

2 parts rosemary	4 parts basil	4 parts parsley
2 parts thyme	2 parts oregano	1 part sage

PESTO AND PROSCIUTTO APPETIZER PIZZA

Traditional Italian flavors of basil and prosciutto blend to make a savory pie.

Suggested crust: 8 oz. Italian style
½ cup pesto cream sauce (see page 50)
2 oz. diced prosciutto
4 oz. shredded mozzarella
1 oz. grated Asiago

Using your fingertips, hand-stretch the pizza dough to 12" and place on a cornmeal-dusted peel. Spread sauce onto crust, sprinkle on 2 oz. diced prosciutto. Top with shredded mozzarella and sprinkle on grated Asiago. Bake at 500° F for about 8 minutes, until cheese is melted and crust begins to brown. Serve cut into squares.

NOTES

—You might be tempted to add more ingredients or even increase the amount of prosciutto, but keep this one simple—lots of flavors to savor just the way it is.

—This pie makes a nice appetizer pizza, but a 12 oz. dough stretched medium thick makes a slightly heartier pie, if you want to serve it in slices as an entrée.

—If you can't find diced prosciutto, use the more commonly found thin slices and cut them into strips. Pancetta is another option.

SUN-DRIED TOMATO APPETIZER PIZZA

A thin-crust pie with intense flavors and interesting textures, just right to start off a meal.

Recommended crust: 8 oz. Italian style

½ cup Mornay sauce (see page 46)

½ cup sun-dried tomatoes

¼ cup sliced almonds

2 or 3 large leaves of fresh basil, cut into strips

Using your fingertips, hand-stretch the pizza dough to 12" to 14" and place on a cornmeal-dusted peel. Top with Mornay sauce and sun-dried tomatoes, then sprinkle on almonds. Bake at 500° F for about 10 minutes, or until almonds are toasted and crust begins to brown. Remove from oven and garnish with basil.

NOTES

—This is the first "white pizza" I ever tasted, at a restaurant in Louisville, Kentucky, in the late 1980s, and I immediately fell in love with the flavors and textures of this pie. If you are trying to serve something different to finicky or timid pizza eaters, this is a good start.

—This truly is an appetizer pizza—not enough to satisfy, but just enough to take the edge off your hunger. I recommend a "party cut" (i.e., squares rather than slices) so the serving size stays small.

—Try different combinations of cheeses for your Mornay sauce. I like Parmesan and white cheddar, but Swiss, Emmentaler, Gruyère, Fontina, Romano, and even Gorgonzola are all possibilities.

TOASTED CHEESE APPETIZERS

Okay, not really a pizza, but nice for guests to nosh on while you are making sauce.

1 12" narrow baguette, slightly stale
1 cup grated Asiago cheese, or a mixture of cheeses
⅓ cup mayonnaise
¼ cup chopped garlic chives
1 Tbs. each fresh minced parsley, oregano, and basil
¼ tsp. ground pepper

Preheat broiler. Slice the baguette into ½-inch slices on the diagonal— go ahead and eat the ends—and set aside. Combine remaining ingredients in a small bowl and stir until thoroughly mixed. Spread the cheese mixture on the bread slices and arrange them on an ungreased baking sheet. Broil until the cheese is melted, bubbly, and slightly browned. Serve while hot.

NOTES

—I first made these appetizers for our annual Memorial Day picnic and they were a huge hit—Br. Nathaniel was eating them like they were potato chips! That day I used homemade French bread, but you could use bakery bread if you absolutely have to. When I taught my friend Lynette to make these, we used homemade sourdough onion bread—mmm!

—Experiment with different cheeses and herbs. I've made these with white cheddar, sage, parsley, and chives and they were quite good.

—If you don't have fresh herbs, use dried, but reduce the chives to 2 tablespoons and the other herbs to 1 teaspoon each.

Pizzas

ASPARAGUS MORNAY PIZZA

A delicious cheese sauce perfectly accents the ham and asparagus in this gourmet pie topped with Swiss.

Recommended crust: 12–14 oz. American or Italian style
1 pound young asparagus spears
1 cup chicken stock or broth
½ cup Mornay sauce (see page 46)
2 oz. sliced black olives
4 oz. ham, diced or cut into strips
4–6 oz. Swiss cheese

Rinse asparagus spears and cut them into 6" lengths; use the top halves and save the bottom halves to make soup. Bring 1 cup of chicken stock to boil over medium heat in a large skillet with a lid. Lower heat to medium and add the asparagus spears. Cover and let steam for 2 minutes. Remove from heat and drain off liquid immediately.

Roll or stretch dough out to 12" to 14" and place on a pizza peel dusted with cornmeal. Spread sauce on the crust and top with ham. Arrange asparagus like spokes on a wheel with the spear tips facing outward. Sprinkle 2 oz. of sliced olives over all, and top with shredded Swiss cheese, or slices torn into small pieces.

NOTES

—I have made this pizza for monks, teenagers, culinary students, and guests at a fancy wine party and everyone has loved it, even some people who don't care for asparagus. It might be a good way to introduce a new vegetable to children—if they won't eat it, at least fake disappointment as you devour it all yourself.

—The steaming of the asparagus in chicken stock adds a nice flavor and softens the asparagus slightly, but this step isn't absolutely necessary. By the way, use this method of parboiling asparagus, broccoli, or cauliflower in chicken stock when you are serving these vegetables as a side dish and you won't need a cheese sauce or much additional seasoning.

—The arrangement of the asparagus necessitates a wedge cut rather than squares. If you are serving this as an appetizer, consider cutting the asparagus into 1" to 2" pieces and spreading them evenly. Then you can make smaller square portions, also known as a "party cut."

BROCCOLI CHICKEN PIZZA

A velouté sauce complements diced chicken, broccoli florets, black olives, and fresh mozzarella.

Recommended crust: 12–14 oz. American or Italian style
1 grilled chicken breast, diced
¾ cup velouté sauce (see page 56)
2 cups coarsely chopped broccoli florets
⅓ cup sliced black olives
12 oz. fresh mozzarella

Roll or stretch dough out to 12" to 14" and place on a pizza peel dusted with cornmeal. Spread velouté sauce over dough, then top with chicken, broccoli, and olives. Tear mozzarella into small pieces and distribute evenly over top. Bake on a preheated pizza stone at 500° F until the cheese is melted and the crust is lightly browned.

NOTES

—A <u>very</u> popular pizza at my Stage Rat pizza fund-raisers. I usually use the American-style crust, but the Italian will work just fine, too.

—You can put the broccoli florets on raw, or you can blanch them lightly using the same method as described for Asparagus Mornay Pizza, on page 72.

—½ cup may not seem like a lot of sauce, but the fresh mozzarella is so creamy when it melts that you won't need too much more. It's easiest to tear the mozz into pieces if you cut it into thick slices first.

CARBONARA PIZZA

A traditional Italian bacon called "guanciale" is used to make this carbonara pizza.

Recommended crust: 14 oz. American style, either fresh or par-baked
8 oz. of guanciale, chopped
1 Tbs. reserved bacon fat
1 Tbs. flour
1 cup heavy cream
3 oz. shredded Pecorino Romano
1 egg
Small bundle of green onions, coarsely chopped
Ground pepper

Cook the guanciale over medium heat until just crisp and drain, reserving 1 Tbs. of the fat. Set aside guanciale. In a small saucepan over medium-low heat, combine bacon fat and flour and cook until lightly browned, whisking constantly to form a roux. Add the whipping cream and whisk gently until slightly thickened, being careful to simmer but not boil the mixture. Add the Romano and whisk until smooth; remove from heat. In a separate bowl, beat the egg and add a small amount of the sauce to temper the egg before whisking it into the sauce. If the sauce seems too thick, whisk in a small amount of milk. Fold in the drained and chopped bacon.

Roll dough out into a 12" to 14" crust with a thicker outer edge. Place on a pizza peel well dusted with cornmeal; par-bake, if desired. Spread the sauce evenly on the crust and top with chopped green onions. Season lightly with ground pepper. Bake on a preheated pizza stone at 500° F until the crust is lightly browned.

NOTES

—This is the pie that convinced my publisher to do this pizza cookbook. I served it at a charity fund-raiser he had organized, and he said it might actually be the best pizza he's ever eaten. Make it and decide for yourself.

—Guanciale is a traditional Italian bacon especially popular in Umbria. It is an un-smoked bacon prepared from the cheek or jowl of the hog—in the U.S. it is sometimes called jowl bacon. It has a stronger flavor than the usual breakfast bacon, but also a unique quality to the fat that makes this sauce silky smooth. It can be hard to find (but worth the search!), but pancetta can be substituted with slightly different results.

—I have made this as presented here, and I have made it with less expensive ingredients like half and half, ordinary bacon, and cheaper domestic cheese, and believe me, there is a HUGE difference. Treat yourself to the good stuff, or stick with sausage and pepperoni!

—You can also use the Italian-style crusts (medium thickness rather than thin) and divide the sauce between several smaller pizzas.

DENVER DINER PIZZA

Everything that goes in a Denver omelet—including the eggs!

Recommended crust: 14 oz. American style

$1/3$ cup Béchamel sauce

$1/2$ cup each diced ham and tomato

$1/4$ cup each chopped green pepper and onion

1 cup shredded cheddar cheese

3 cups shredded mozzarella

5 or 6 raw eggs

Roll dough out into a 12" to 14" crust with a thicker outer edge. Place on a pizza peel well dusted with cornmeal. Brush on Béchamel sauce, then top with ham, tomato, onion, and peppers. Sprinkle cheddar cheese on top, then the mozzarella. Bake on a pizza stone in a preheated 500° F oven for 3 minutes—just long enough to get the mozzarella to begin to melt. Spray the bottom of a cup or glass with non-stick spray and press five or six divots into the half-melted cheese; crack an egg into each divot. Carefully slide back into the oven and bake until eggs are over-easy.

NOTES

—I developed this recipe for a PBS event in Denver and was astonished by how good an egg pizza could taste! This has become one of my favorite recipes, and it is often requested by guests at my pizza parties.

—To serve, bring the pizza out to the table whole, so your family and friends can appreciate its unusual appearance. Then stir the yolks and whites together and spread over the top of the entire pizza, salt and pepper the whole mess, and cut it into squares.

—One warning: If your oven doesn't cook evenly, be sure to rotate the pizza once or twice during the baking period, or you could end up with hard-cooked eggs on one side and runny on the other. Also, the eggs will still jiggle back and forth quite a bit even when over-easy, so be careful not to overcook them. Just make sure all the whites are opaque and you should be just fine in terms of texture and food safety. Another option—less fun but also less risky—is to cook the eggs ahead of time in a skillet and simply slide them onto the pizza or even onto individual servings. But if you want pizza without risk, maybe you should just order delivery!

PIZZA DIAVOLO

A devilishly hot pizza, with sauce laced with Tabasco, hot sausage, onions, extra spicy giardiniera, jalapeños, mozzarella, and pepper jack cheeses.

Recommended crust: 14 oz. American style
½ cup pizza sauce
1–2 Tbs. Tabasco or other hot sauce
4 oz. shredded pepper jack cheese
½ pound hot link sausage, cooked and sliced into rounds
½ medium yellow onion, coarsely chopped
½ cup extra spicy giardiniera, chopped
¼ cup jalapeño slices
8 oz. shredded mozzarella
Dried crushed red peppers or cayenne powder

Roll crust out to 12" to 14" and dock the dough. Place on a pizza peel well dusted with cornmeal. Mix pizza sauce and hot sauce, spread evenly over crust, and top with pepper jack cheese, followed by sausage, onion, giardiniera, and jalapeños, in that order. Spread mozzarella over all, and sprinkle with red pepper or cayenne powder. Bake pizza on a preheated stone at 500° F for about 10 minutes, or until cheese begins to brown lightly. Keep a fire extinguisher handy in case the pizza spontaneously combusts upon removal from oven.

NOTES

—Our Br. Robert hails from Texas and puts hot sauce on everything but breakfast cereal. I developed this "devil pizza" to please his Tex-Mex palate, and it's proved to be a favorite with other lovers of spicy foods.

—How spicy-hot this pizza gets depends in large part on the hot sauce you use. Whole sections of some supermarkets are dedicated to hot sauces with evocative (or provocative) names, each one spicier than the last. I once tried one that was so hot, I'm not sure what I was supposed to taste besides pain.

—Giardiniera is a pickled blend of onions, cauliflower, carrots, and peppers and is usually found in the same supermarket section as the olives. The mild version makes a nice pizza topping as well.

—A reminder about cooking sausage for pizza—be very careful not to over cook since the sausage gets heated again on the pizza. An instant-read thermometer is useful here: at least 160° F, nothing above 170° F.

ḦOT ITALIAN ṢAUṢAGE

Just in case you want to make your own bulk sausage, here's my favorite recipe.

1 lb. ground pork
2 tsp. Italian herb blend
1½ tsp. garlic powder
1½ tsp. fennel seed
½ tsp celery salt
1 tsp crushed red pepper
2 tsp. black pepper
¾ tsp. salt

Mix thoroughly in a bowl, cover, and refrigerate until use.

NOTES

—Sausage is often made with ground pork butt, but you can use leaner cuts as well and have the butcher grind it for you. I often order five pounds of ground pork wrapped in one-pound packages and keep them in the freezer for Thursday nights.

—I usually place all the seasonings in a pestle and crush it with a mortar before adding it to the meat. You could also run it through a spice grinder. The result is a more even taste to the sausage, without one bite being seriously hotter than the next.

—Having gotten miserably ill on a road trip because of some bad Chinese food, I worry about food safety. So I generally brown this sausage before using it on pizza. Don't cook it too dry, and try not to break up the meat like you would for chili or sloppy joes—leave the pieces a bit bigger so you get real meaty texture in a bite. Like my friend Josh says, "I don't want my sausage looking like rabbit poop."

—The heat here comes from garlic and two kinds of pepper. You can experiment with increasing and / or decreasing one or the other to "fine-tune" the flavor.

FOUR CHEESE TOMATO-TOP PIZZA

A blend of Italian cheeses mixed with herbs and topped with garden tomatoes—simple, beautiful, delicious.

Recommended crust: 14 oz. American style

6 oz. shredded mozzarella

4 oz. ricotta

2 oz. shredded provolone

2 oz. grated Romano

1 egg

½ tsp. nutmeg

¼ cup fresh snipped chives or garlic chives

16 to 24 slices of plum tomato

Drain tomato slices on paper towels for about 15 minutes. Roll dough out to 12" to 14" with a thicker raised edge and place on a pizza peel dusted with cornmeal. In a medium-size bowl, combine cheeses with egg, nutmeg, and chives. Mix with hands until thoroughly blended. Spread cheese mixture evenly over pizza crust and arrange tomato slices on top. Bake in a preheated 500° F oven for 10–15 minutes, or until cheese starts to brown lightly. Salt and pepper lightly if desired.

NOTES

—*This is one of my favorite pizzas, especially when we have fresh tomatoes. The plum tomatoes are best, because they have more flesh and less juice, but other tomatoes work fine if you drain the slices on paper towels for at least 30 minutes before use. You can, of course, make this pizza without tomatoes, if you want a classic Quattro Formaggi pie—use an Italian-style crust.*

—*Try to get a strongly flavored, well-aged provolone, and don't be afraid to ask the deli worker for samples. You can also experiment with other cheeses (Parmesan, Asiago, Fontina, Gorgonzola, etc.) or vary proportions. I make this pizza differently every time, depending upon what's in the fridge and/or in the garden, and I'm never disappointed.*

—*If I make this pie for Thursday night haustus, I always make it last, in the hopes that leftovers will return to the kitchen, because this pizza is just about the best cold breakfast I have ever had.*

ITALIAN BEEF PIZZA

Recommended crust: 14 oz. American style, either fresh or par-baked
$\frac{1}{3}$ cup pizza sauce
6 to 8 oz. thinly sliced deli-style Italian beef or garlic beef
1 each of red, green, and yellow pepper, julienned
1 red onion, julienned
4 oz. smoked mozzarella, shredded
6 to 9 slices of provolone, torn into pieces
Olive oil

Lightly sauté peppers and onion in a little olive oil. Roll crust out
to 12" to 14" with a slightly raised outer edge. Place on a pizza peel
dusted with cornmeal; par-bake if a crisper crust is desired. Spread the
crust with a light layer of pizza sauce, then sprinkle the smoked mozzarella evenly over the sauce. Cut or pull apart the deli beef into strips.
Then layer the beef, onions, and peppers on the crust in that order,
and top with pieces of provolone. Bake pizza on a preheated stone
at 500° F for about 10 minutes, or until provolone begins to brown
lightly at the edges.

NOTES

—I find that this pizza is especially popular with guys watching a sporting event, no matter what the season! Having flavorful beef is especially important, so if you can't find anything good at the deli counter of your local grocery, try to find an authentic Italian butcher nearby, or experiment with making your own in a slow cooker or Crock-pot. The trick to thin slices, apart from having a professional-grade deli slicer at home, is to put homemade Italian beef in the freezer for a couple of hours before you slice it. A couple Internet sites that might help: http://www.amazingribs.com/recipes/beef/italian_beef.html and http://thepauperedchef.com/2009/02/homemade-italian-beef.html.

—I know it is customary for the peppers and onions to be overcooked and limp in most Italian beef sandwiches, but avoid that temptation here. A light sauté is all that is called for, as they will cook further on the pizza, and a slight crunch left in the peppers adds to the textural delights of this pizza—better "mouth feel" as they say in culinary school.

—The layer of smoked mozzarella under the beef gives this pie a wonderfully smoky flavor. Using torn pieces of provolone makes for a more beautiful presentation—the colors of the peppers really come through—so this is the pizza I make when I need to do some kind of TV appearance. But I have also made this pie without the smoked mozz, and simply topped the whole pie with overlapping whole slices of provolone.

KIDS' PIZZA CUPS

A fun pizza project for kids from preschool to high school.

1 pkg. fast-rising yeast
1 Tbs. granulated sugar
1 tsp. salt
3 to 3½ cups all-purpose flour, divided
1 cup skim milk
1 Tbs. vegetable oil
Pizza toppings (see below)

In a medium-size mixing bowl, sift together yeast, sugar, and salt, along with 2 cups of flour. Heat milk to 120 to 130° F. Pour milk and oil into flour mixture and stir until well blended. Add another cup of flour and mix with your hands until flour is thoroughly incorporated. Add remaining flour about 1 tablespoon at a time, until a soft dough is formed that pulls away from the sides of the bowl. Turn out onto a lightly floured board and knead for 5 minutes, adding more flour as needed to keep dough manageable. When finished, the dough should be slightly soft but should spring back when pushed. Cover dough with a damp towel and let rest for 10 minutes. The dough is then ready to use.

Preheat oven to 425° F, and lightly grease two Texas-size muffin tins. Divide dough into 12 pieces. Roll each piece into a circle 6" in diameter and use to line the individual muffin cups—the dough should come about ¾ of the way up the sides. Layer each mini-deep dish pizza as follows:

2 Tbs. grated mozzarella cheese

1 Tbs. pizza sauce

2 Tbs. other toppings (sausage, peppers, onions, etc.)

1 more Tbs. pizza sauce

1 more Tbs. cheese

Bake at 425° F for 12 to 15 minutes, until crust is browned and cheese is melted and slightly browned. Allow to set in pan for 5 minutes before serving. Makes 12 mini-pizzas.

NOTES

—These pizza cups are ideal for a kids' party, because they're fast to make—dough is ready in 20 minutes, and they only bake for 15. Better still, each child can choose the toppings he or she wants. No more fighting over who wants onions and who wants pepperoni! Kids love helping with this recipe—the older ones can make the dough, while little ones can roll out the dough or fill the cups.

—To make it easier to form the individual cups, drape the rolled-out circle of dough over an inverted 1 cup measure and press to form the appropriate shape. Use the handle of the measuring cup to turn it over into the muffin tin, remove measuring cup, and then press dough to the sides of the tin. Try it—it's easy and fast!

—You can use regular muffin tins, but they hold so little that they're more like hors d'oeuvres, and that seems like a lot of fuss to me.

—A pound of grated cheese and an 8 oz. can of pizza sauce is enough for 12 pizza cups. The amounts of the other toppings are variable, depending on how much you use of each—a pound of browned sausage is ample, for example. If you use pepperoni, cut the slices into quarters first, and be sure to chop vegetables smaller than usual.

PIZZA MARGHERICA

A classic pie that is both rustic and elegant in its simplicity: tomato, cheese, basil.

Recommended crust: 8–12 oz. Italian style
4 large plum tomatoes, diced and drained
1 garlic clove, mashed and minced
3 or 4 large leaves of fresh basil, cut into strips
½ pound fresh mozzarella, torn into pieces

Using your fingertips, hand-stretch the pizza dough to 12" to 14" and place on a cornmeal-dusted peel. Toss diced tomatoes with garlic. Top the dough with the diced tomatoes and the fresh mozzarella. Bake on a preheated pizza stone at 500° F until the crust is lightly browned and the mozzarella is fully melted. Remove from oven and top with basil before serving.

NOTES

—This is considered the grandmother of all modern pizzas. The story is that in 1889, King Umberto of Italy was vacationing in Naples with his lovely wife, Margherita, when they grew tired of haute cuisine and asked a local pizzaiolo named Raffaele Esposito to make them dinner. He created a pizza with red tomatoes, white mozzarella, and green basil—the colors of the Italian flag—and named it for the queen on the spot. Charming as this sounds, such pizzas were common enough throughout Italy since the mid-eighteenth century, so it's unlikely Esposito "invented" it. But when the queen sent a letter of praise, he was a savvy enough businessman to capitalize on it by naming it after her somewhat after the fact.

—You can also make this pizza with the 8-minute sauce on page 39, but use a can of diced tomatoes instead of crushed.

—The variation in the amount of dough depends upon whether you want a thin or medium-thick crust. In any case, use a traditional Italian hand-stretching technique for this classic pie. If you have smaller basil leaves, say from a "Fine Verde" or "Spicy Globe" basil, use whole leaves sprinkled evenly over the pie.

MUFFALECTA PIZZA

Inspired by the New Orleans sandwich, this pie is a meat lover's dream come true, especially if you also like garlic and olives.

Recommended crust: 14 oz. American style, either fresh or par-baked
¼ cup pizza sauce (optional)
1 cup olive salad
3 to 4 oz. each capocola, mortadella, and Genoa salami slices, cut into strips
8 to 10 oz. shredded mozzarella and provolone cheese blend

Roll dough out into a 12" to 14" crust with a thicker outer edge. Place on a pizza peel well dusted with cornmeal; par-bake if desired. Spread pizza sauce evenly over the crust if desired. Layer the olive salad, meats, and cheese in that order, and bake pizza on a preheated stone at 500° F for about 10–12 minutes, or until cheese begins to brown very lightly.

NOTES

—*The muffaletta is a sandwich made popular in New Orleans by Italian immigrants. Originally the name was associated with a round loaf of bread but has become synonymous with a sandwich made with Italian deli meats and cheeses with a garlic olive salad condiment.*

—*The cappocola and salami should be sliced thin before being cut into strips; the mortadella should be a medium-thick slice. You can lay whole slices on the pizza instead of cutting the strips, but I find it easier to eat if the pieces are a bit smaller.*

—*Another option for the cheese is to take whole round slices of provolone and lay them over the pizza, slightly overlapping, which gives the pie an interesting appearance. Remember that provolone won't brown as much as mozz, so don't over bake.*

OLIVE SALAD

¾ cup medium pimiento-stuffed green olives

2 or 3 large garlic cloves, mashed and minced

1 Tbs. balsamic vinegar or red wine vinegar

½ cup medium black olives

½ cup Italian mild giardiniera

1 Tbs. fresh minced Italian parsley

¼ cup minced red onion

2 Tbs. capers, drained

1 Tbs. fresh minced oregano

½ tsp. red pepper flakes

2 Tbs. olive oil

1 Tbs. grated Parmesan

Drain and coarsely chop the green olives, black olives, and giardiniera, and combine them in a bowl. Add remaining ingredients, give it a couple of twists from the pepper mill and toss until blended. Cover bowl and refrigerate until use.

NOTES

—*This is the traditional condiment on a New Orleans muffaletta sandwich, although some recipes have more ingredients: thinly sliced celery, roasted red peppers, artichoke hearts, etc. I simplified by using giardiniera (an Italian mix of cauliflower, carrots, celery, peppers, etc., usually pickled). You can experiment with whatever is at the market or coming out of your garden at the moment.*

—*You can use this as a topping for the Muffaletta Pizza, as a topping by itself on an Italian-style crust or focaccia, or scooped up with crostini. If you like olives, you'll think of any number of ways to use it!*

PARMESAN CREAM AND SCALLOPS PIZZA

Scallops in a rich sauce that is a snap to make.

Recommended crust: 14 oz. American style, fresh or par-baked
½ cup Parmesan cream sauce (see page 48)
½ pound bay scallops
1 medium garlic clove, mashed and minced
1 Tbs. olive oil
Sliced almonds (optional)

Roll dough out to a 12" to 14" round with a slightly raised outer edge. Place on a pizza peel well dusted with cornmeal; par-bake if desired. In a small saucepan, sauté garlic in a little olive oil for about 1 minute. Add bay scallops and sauté lightly until they just begin to turn opaque—do not over cook. Remove from heat. Spread sauce on dough and distribute scallops evenly over pizza. If desired, top with sliced almonds. Bake pizza on a preheated stone at 500° F for about 10 minutes, or until sauce begins to brown lightly and scallops are cooked through.

NOTES

—I served my first scallop pizza to a group of volunteers who had come out to decorate our school gym for an event. The recipe was both a success and a failure: everyone said the pizza was excellent and insisted I had to go make another, after which everyone was so full that no more work got done on the project for the rest of the evening!

—For the crust, the cornmeal variation works well for this pizza (see page 31). If you decide to try an Italian-style crust, reduce the amount of sauce or you could get a rather soggy center.

—I suspect any number of other kinds of seafood could be used with this sauce, including clams or lumped crab.

—You can use raw scallops if they are small enough, but I feel a bit safer by sautéing them just a bit first. If you have sea scallops, cut them into smaller pieces. I have used both fresh and thawed frozen scallops with success.

ROTOLA PIZZA

You'll love both the appearance and the flavor of this simple but unique pizza.

Recommended crust: 12–14 oz. Italian style
½ to ¾ cup 8-minute pizza sauce (see page 39)
2 8-oz. packages of Prosciutto Rotola

Using your fingertips, hand-stretch the pizza dough to 12" to 14" and place on a cornmeal-dusted peel. Dock the dough if desired. Spread pizza sauce evenly. Cut Rotola into ½" slices and arrange on top of sauce. Bake pizza on a preheated stone at 500° F for about 10–12 minutes, or until cheese melts and prosciutto has cooked.

NOTES

—A product of Volpi Meats, Inc., Rotola is made of thick slices of mozzarella topped with prosciutto and rolled up like a jelly roll. They are available even in my local small-town market, but if you can't find them you can make your own if your local deli has blocks of mozzarella that you can have sliced.

—I know this is a ridiculously simple recipe, but most people serve sliced Rotola on top of crostini for antipasti or on raw tomatoes put under a broiler, so you might not think of using them for a pie. But a Rotola Pizza gives you pools of melted mozz with a crisp spiral of prosciutto ham in the center—you'll love it! The Rotola are also available with basil, sun-dried tomato, and salami.

—If you want a bit more crunch, par-bake the crust for about 3 minutes before adding the toppings.

SEAFOOD PIZZA

A little extra work, a lot of ingredients—and an exquisite pie with complex flavors and textures.

Recommended crust: 12 oz. Italian style
6 oz. tiny shrimp, cleaned and cooked
4 oz. cooked crab meat
Béchamel sauce (see page 42)
1 tsp. instant vegetable bouillon base
½ cup sliced celery
¼ cup chopped onions
10 small slices mushrooms
3 oz. chèvre cheese
6 oz. shredded mozzarella
Salt and pepper to taste

Make Béchamel sauce and whisk in vegetable bouillon base until smooth. Set aside to cool slightly. Using your fingertips, hand-stretch the pizza dough to 12" to 14" and place on a cornmeal-dusted peel. Spread on about half of the Béchamel sauce—reserve the remainder for other use. Top with shrimp, crab, and vegetables. Crumble or cut chèvre into small pieces and sprinkle evenly over the other ingredients, and top with the shredded mozzarella. Bake at 500° F on a preheated pizza stone for about 10 minutes or until crust is lightly browned and cheese is melted. Season to taste.

NOTES

—I first created this pie when I gave a pizza party for the female boarding students of our high school. Many of them are Asian and love any kind of seafood, so this dish must have been especially popular with them, because they keep asking me when their next party will be!

—The vegetable bouillon base referred to here is the paste that comes in a jar. I keep chicken and beef base in the pantry all the time as well. Sometimes they can be a little salty, so be careful with your seasoning. If you have a favorite recipe for a sherry cream sauce, it would work well here, too.

—If you're not fond of chèvre or other goat cheese, you might try ricotta or Monterey Jack, or even substitute Mornay sauce for the vegetable-flavored Béchamel. A light garnish of paprika wouldn't hurt, either.

SMOKED SALMON PIZZA

The crust is baked first like a focaccia and the ingredients put on when it's cold.

Recommended crust: 14 oz. Italian style
Olive oil
8 oz. pkg. cream cheese, room temperature
2 Tbs. capers
3 to 4 Tbs. fresh dill (about 20 small sprigs)
8 to 12 oz. smoked salmon

Using your fingertips, hand-stretch the pizza dough to 12". Place crust on a cornmeal-dusted peel and cover with a clean, dry towel. Allow dough to rise for 20 minutes. Press your fingertip to make dimples all over the dough. Brush the top of the dough with olive oil and slide dough onto a preheated pizza stone at 450° F. Bake for 12–14 minutes or until browned (the interior temperature of the bread should be 190° F to 195° F). Remove from oven with peel and allow to cool to lukewarm.

Spread cream cheese over top of warm crust. Sprinkle with capers. Break the salmon into pieces with a fork and distribute evenly over cheese and garnish with dill sprigs.

NOTES

——This pizza was taste-tested at a gourmet pizza and wine pairing party at a fine little restaurant called the Nodding Onion in Utica, Illinois. The owner, Kevin Ryan, is a former student of mine and lets me use the restaurant for pizza party fund-raisers for our drama department. He smoked the salmon himself, which certainly added to the quality of the finished product, but you can let your local deli do the job for you, too.

——We discovered that this pizza pairs nicely with white wines that are dry and have some acidity (try a white Bordeaux, avoid oaked Chardonnays), and if reds are your preference go for a Pinot Noir.

——Onions are another traditional ingredient to accompany smoked salmon. Feel free to add them here, but only in very thin slices or they can overwhelm the other flavors. You can also use the onion crust variation (see page 31).

SPINACH PESTO PIZZA

You'll love the bright green of the spinach pesto for this pie, which has fresh vegetable flavors and a gourmet appearance.

Recommended crust: 8 oz. Italian style
⅓ cup spinach pesto
2 thin slices of red onion, sections divided
2 or 3 baby portabella mushrooms, sliced
3 oz. shredded Muenster cheese (without rind)

Using your fingertips, hand-stretch the pizza dough to 8" to 10" and place on a cornmeal-dusted peel. Spread spinach pesto evenly over the dough, leaving about a ½" border at the edge. Evenly distribute onion and mushrooms over pesto, and sprinkle with cheese. Bake at 500° F on a preheated pizza stone for about 10 minutes, or until cheese is bubbly and slightly browned.

NOTES

—I developed this pizza one haustus night when we had a large pan of spinach left over from lunch. I had seen a lot of spinach pizza recipes that used cooked, frozen, or canned spinach (gak!), but the appearance of the fresh spinach leaves reminded me so much of basil that I thought of concocting a spinach pesto instead. The shredded Muenster was inspired by leftovers as well, so feel free to try other cheeses.

—You can certainly make a larger pizza than the one suggested here with more toppings, but I like these proportions best.

SPICY THAI PEANUT CHICKEN PIZZA

A typically American dish, with a mash-up of flavors and techniques from different cultures.

Recommended crust: 12–14 oz. American style

¾ cup spicy peanut sauce

1 grilled chicken breast, diced

1 red pepper, sliced into strips

3 green onions, chopped

8 to 12 oz. shredded fontina

Roll dough out into a 12" to 14" crust with a slightly thicker outer edge. Place on a pizza peel well dusted with cornmeal. Spread with peanut sauce and top with chicken, pepper, and onion. Cover with shredded fontina. Bake on a preheated pizza stone at 500° F until the crust is lightly browned and cheese is melted. Do not allow the cheese to brown too much or else the chicken will dry out.

NOTES

—Traditional Thai chefs probably feel about this pie the way I feel about taco pizzas—"What were you thinking?" But even though this is neither authentic Thai nor the least bit Italian, the blend of the two cultures seems to work well for a lot of people.

—California Pizza Kitchen made this popular—their version includes a sprinkling of roasted peanuts on the top (a nice touch), as well as shredded carrot and bean sprouts, neither of which particularly appeals to me. And if you have to put on fresh cilantro, please don't tell me about it—can't stand the stuff.

—This is my sister Lisa's favorite pizza, and she is constantly dropping hints about making it for her. Maybe now that I've shared the recipe she'll stop bugging me—but I wouldn't count on it!

—It can be hard to pair wines with Asian flavors, but here's a couple of guidelines: avoid oaked wines or anything too tannic, look for fruity flavors, and don't be afraid to try sparkling wines if they aren't too dry. Or try a malt lager or a lime-flavored beer.

STAGE RAT-A-TOUILLE PIZZA

Not only is this pizza delicious, it is absolutely beautiful coming out of the oven and to the table. Impress your veggie-loving guests with this gourmet beauty, and serve it with a light red wine.

Recommended crust: 12 oz. Italian style
½ cup cubed eggplant
10 to 12 thin zucchini slices
1 small yellow squash, julienned
½ small red onion, halved and sliced
1 garlic clove, mashed and minced
Olive oil
⅓ cup chopped tomatoes
2 Tbs. tomato paste
8 oz. shredded mozzarella or cheese blend

Stretch dough out to 12" to 14". Place on a peel well dusted with cornmeal and set aside. Over medium-high heat, sauté vegetables and garlic in olive oil for about 2 minutes. Add chopped tomatoes and tomato paste and stir until blended. Remove from heat and distribute mixture over pizza crust (you may not use all of it). Top with cheese and bake at 500° F on a preheated pizza stone for about 10 minutes, or until cheese is bubbly and slightly browned.

NOTES

—Our high school technical theatre crew is known as the "Stage Rats" and since I am both the Head Rat and a pizza chef, the Disney film **Ratatouille** is naturally one of my favorite films. When we had a pizza fund-raiser for the drama department, I developed this recipe with lightly sautéed Mediterranean vegetables, which are like ratatouille on a tender pizza crust.

—The actual French dish ratatouille is much more carefully constructed with regard to the order in which the vegetables enter the skillet, but since this goes into the oven as well, I've simplified things a bit.

—Do not attempt this recipe with a larger or older eggplant, which will likely add a bitter flavor. Keep an eye out for younger, smaller ones both in the local market and in your garden.

DESSERTS

APPLE PIE PIZZA

A sweet crust, topped with apricot butter, sautéed apples, and pecans.

14 oz. sweet crust (see page 34)

3 Tbs. butter

4 or 5 medium tart apples, peeled, cored, quartered, and sliced

½ cup brown sugar

1 tsp. ground cinnamon

¼ tsp. salt

½ cup apricot butter or preserves

½ cup chopped pecans

In a large skillet, melt butter over medium heat. Add apples and toss to coat. Sauté apples for 5 to 8 minutes, occasionally turning them over gently. Sprinkle on brown sugar, cinnamon, and salt. Continue to stir gently as the sugar dissolves and caramelizes slightly. When apples are slightly soft but not mushy, remove from heat and allow to cool slightly. Prepare crust by rolling dough out to 12" to 14" and placing on a flour-dusted pizza peel. Dock the crust to prevent large air bubbles (see page 13). Bake on a preheated pizza stone at 425° F for 4 minutes. Remove from oven and spread with apricot preserves, top evenly with apple mixture, and sprinkle on chopped pecans. Bake for an additional 8 to 10 minutes or until the crust is golden brown and apple mixture is bubbling. Remove from oven and allow to settle slightly before cutting. Serve warm with a little whipped cream on top.

NOTES

—This pie to <u>so</u> much better than those sticky sweet cinnamon-and-frosting dessert pizzas served at pizza chains everywhere. The hardest job for this pie is having to prepare the apple slices, but it's a small price to pay for the delicious result. As with any apple pie, the size and thickness of the slices are up to you.

—There is a little more butter than needed for the sauté, but it helps once the brown sugar is added.

—If you cheat and use canned pie filling for this pizza, you have to go to confession afterward.

FIG AND PAPAYA DESSERT PIZZA

A sweet crust with sweetened lemon cream cheese mixed with Kadota fig preserves and topped with dried figs and papaya.

12 oz. sweet crust
4 oz. cream cheese, room temperature
Juice and zest of 1 small lemon
¼ to ⅓ cup powdered sugar
½ cup Kadota fig preserves
½ cup chopped dried Calmyra figs
½ cup chopped dried papaya or mango
French vanilla ice cream
Sugared pecans or other honey-roasted nuts

In a small bowl, combine cream cheese with zest and juice of lemon and powdered sugar and whisk until smooth—start with ¼ cup of powdered sugar and add more to taste as needed. Fold in fig preserves until consistency of mixture is even. Set aside. Prepare crust by rolling dough out to 12" to 14" and placing on a flour-dusted pizza peel. Dock the crust to prevent large air bubbles (see page 13). Bake on a preheated pizza stone at 425° F for 4 minutes. Remove from oven and spread with cream cheese mixture, top evenly with chopped figs and papaya. Bake for an additional 8 to 10 minutes or until the crust is golden brown and cream cheese mixture begins to brown slightly. Remove from oven and allow to cool slightly before cutting. Serve warm with a small dollop of French vanilla ice cream and garnish ice cream with nuts.

NOTES

—This dessert has proved to be the runaway favorite at gourmet pizza fund-raisers and informal parties. I made it once for some of our boarding students and the house mother warned, "Don't change a thing about that recipe!"

—It's important to note that "dried" figs and papaya here does not mean "completely dehydrated," but something similar to raisins. If you have a local ethnic grocery, check there for the figs before you go to a big chain supermarket. The price difference can be staggering. I spent $3.49 at my favorite Italian grocery on the Hill in St. Louis for the same amount of figs that cost $11.99 at a Jewel supermarket in my own town.

—Dried papaya can be hard to locate, but Sunsweet makes a dried mango that you can typically find in the same aisle as the raisins.

ABOUT THE AUTHOR

Fr. Dominic Garramone is a Benedictine priest and monk of Saint Bede Abbey in Peru, Illinois. Following a college education in theatre, he entered the monastery in 1983 and was ordained as a priest in 1992. He is well known to public television viewers for his cooking series *Breaking Bread with Father Dominic*, which aired for several years beginning in 1999.

Fr. Dom teaches religion and drama at Saint Bede Academy and is the author of two plays published by Dramatic Publishing, Inc. He is very much in demand as a public speaker at food and wine shows, civic and church groups and retreats, in addition to his monastery's regular weekend parish missions, which he refers to as "Rent-A-Monk."

Fr. Dom describes his culinary education as taking place "between my mother's kitchen and the public library," and he honed his baking and cooking skills by providing bread and pizza for the twenty-five monks of his community. Their favorite haustus pizzas include Four Cheese Tomato Top, Pizza Diavolo, and plain ol' sausage and pepperoni.

OTHER FR. DOMINIC TITLES AVAILABLE FROM REEDY PRESS

'Tis the Season to be Baking:
Christmas Reflections and Bread Recipes
5 x 7
$12.00

Brother Jerome and
the Angels in the Bakery
Illustrated by Richard Bernal
9 x 12
$16.95